HEAL YOU

Simple Words of Wisdom
Gyuto Monks of Tibet

ABC
Books

Published by ABC Enterprises for the
AUSTRALIAN BROADCASTING CORPORATION
GPO Box 9994 Sydney NSW 2001

Copyright © Gyuto House 2003

First published 2003
Reprinted June 2006

National Library of Australia
Cataloguing-in-Publication entry
    Heal your heart: simple words of wisdom from the
    Gyuto monks of Tibet.

    ISBN 10: 0 7333 1256 X

    ISBN 13: 978 0 7333 1256 4

    Meditation – Buddhism. 2. Philosophy, Buddhist.
    3. Buddhism – Doctrines. I. Australian Broadcasting Corporation.

294.34435

Packaged by Limelight Press Pty Ltd
Translation and Script Development: Sonam Rigzin and Maureen Fallon
Project Management: Jayne Denshire
Design: Karen Clark and Susanne Geppert
Colour reproduction by Colorwize Studio, Adelaide
Printed and bound in Singapore through Imago

Foreword

I have spent all my life as a monk, in Tibet until 1959 and since then in India as a refugee with periodic travels to other parts of the world. As I get older, I find, increasingly, that what sustains the human will, in individual or common struggle, is genuine affection.

In the pursuit of a spiritual life and the struggle of the just Tibetan cause, the Gyuto Monks have been fortunate to have encountered that nourishment everywhere. This book is a small but important symbol of gratitude for the kindness and support received.

As simple tantric monks, the basis of our practice is to inspire love for oneself and others as a means of achieving peace and happiness. There is nothing that we value more than this.

May this small book cause those who come across it to experience their own goodness, love and compassion and the clear light of their own innate wisdom.

Lobsang Tsering
GYUTO TANTRIC UNIVERSITY

Lobsang Tsering is appointed to the position of Jangden Chenmo, Great Chantmaster of Gyuto Tantric University, by His Holiness the XIVth Dalai Lama of Tibet.

5

Contents

Monk Gallery

Khensur Rinpoche
Lobsang Tenzin

Lobsang Tsering

Tenzin Sherab
(dec.)

Thupten Kelsang
(dec.)

Jampa Tashi

Thupten Yeshe

Gongkha Tulku
Rinpoche

Tseten Gyurme

Tsultrim Tashi

Tenzin Pempa

Thupten Khedup

Sonam Paljor

Sangey Dhondup

Sonam Rabgye

Lobsang Tsultrim

Dorje Lobsang

Tenzin Cheophal

Thupten Donyo

Thupten Dhundup

Tenzin Karma

Pasang Gyamso

Yeshe Topgyal

Sonam Wanchuk

Tashi Namgyal

Kunchok Rinzin

Yeshe Gyaltsen

Sonam Thinley

Lobsang Tendar

Tsewang Paljor

Tashi Gyamtso

Introduction

Heal Your Heart

These simple words of wisdom from the Gyuto Monks of Tibet offer the essence of Buddhist teaching with a thought or realisation expressed on each page. As you read through each of the three parts, you can absorb the sayings alone, within groups, or sequentially as a journey along the path of life as explained by Buddhist philosophy.

The Gyuto Monks

The monks of Gyuto Tantric University, established in Lhasa, Tibet in 1474, now living in exile in India, are tantric masters who practise the highest form of Buddhist teaching, that of the Vajrayana school, also known as Tantrayana. Experiencing boundless compassion for the suffering of others, their life and their practice is devoted entirely to the urgent goal of enlightenment for the sake of all other living beings. It is a life grounded in artistic endeavour: harmonic chanting, creation of beautiful mandalas in sand, wood or clay, butter sculpting and a myriad of mental and physical ways of practising meditation through visualisation.

To be in the presence of the Gyuto masters as they practise these ancient tantric arts is to be healed and blessed by the blissful energy, the quiet peace and gentle love being expressed on many levels. The Tibetan community places great significance on the Gyuto Monks' ability to conduct healing chants or 'pujas' to assist with all manner of difficulties. In recent years, westerners have benefited also, not only from the tantric arts practices but from the wisdom and compassion of the monks' sayings.

The emphasis in these modest offerings is on love and practice — on being gentle with yourself and acting only from a pure motivation. There is no theory, no therapy, only the opportunity to take a step towards happiness by acting authentically in the moment.

The Mandalas of Gyuto

Sacred within Tibetan Buddhism and, until recently, rarely seen outside the monasteries, mandalas are metaphors for life. Created as ephemeral objects, sand mandalas are reminders of impermanence and non-attachment.

Each is a pictorial manifestation of a tantra or 'teaching' which may be 'read' or used for visualization and meditation leading one to go beyond mental suffering and experience the pure nature of reality. By imagining oneself as a perfect being within a perfect world, one is able to generate innate goodness, creating happiness for oneself and others.

Tantric Transformation through Sound
Gyuto harmonic chanting ~ the Vajrayana approach

Before the chanting sound is actually made, one visualises oneself intensely as a perfect being in the centre of a perfect world. This visualisation clears the mind of everyday emotional and physical attachments allowing a pure perspective. While still in meditation and

using the harmonic deep low chanting as an aid, one begins to move through the energy channels to the heart chakra, that point of very subtle and pure consciousness. The resulting deep harmonic chant vibrates and resonates through the whole body and enables one to transmit a pure and selfless love towards all living beings.

Mandala of Yamantaka

Protector of life and conqueror of our fear of death.

The first teachings

The Buddha Shakyamuni taught Buddhism some 2500 years ago in India based on his own personal experience of the quest for happiness. His teachings present an answer to the problem of unhappiness faced by all human beings. Buddha said, first identify and accept suffering as suffering, define its cause, seek a solution, check the result, and don't live in denial. Then, happiness, the desire of all living beings, is possible.

Buddha presented his teachings in a variety of ways and degrees of complexity, sometimes seeming quite contradictory, to cater to the differing needs of his audience at the time. His teachings, however, broadly fall into three categories, representing the three dominant progressive limits of human intellectual development and capacity. These simple, medium and high level approaches are otherwise known as the three vehicles of Buddhism—Hinayana, Mahayana and Vajrayana. All three schools share the same philosophical premise of achieving happiness. They are differentiated by their understanding of what defines unhappiness, its causes and the means to achieve happiness. They all present this in the form of three divisions: first the base (two truths), then the path (the five stages of evolution), and finally the result (the four states of enlightenment).

Hinayana
~ the simple approach

Hinayana generally believes that the world is the cause of dissatisfaction and adopts rather a narrow and cautious approach by keeping a distance between the self and the world. The belief prefers its followers to be reclusive and concentrate on the practice of mindful meditation and the Eight-fold Noble Path. This existence liberates followers from participation in the world and leads to a so-called nirvana.

The Eight-fold Noble Path

The Eight-fold Path is a way to develop wisdom and discipline through meditation as a framework for seeking enlightenment. Right view and right intention lead to wisdom; right speech, right action and right livelihood create an ethical base; right effort, right mindfulness and right concentration develop the conditions for meditation. According to Hinayana thinking, this set of eight simple guidelines helps you to function safely and effectively in the everyday world without succumbing to temptation.

RIGHT VIEW: understanding of reality including birth, sickness, ageing and death

RIGHT INTENTION: wishing no harm to others

RIGHT SPEECH: speaking truthfully

RIGHT ACTION: abstaining from killing and harmful behaviour

RIGHT LIVELIHOOD: surviving with minimal impact on others

RIGHT EFFORT: diligence and learning from one's mistakes

RIGHT MINDFULNESS: awareness of consequences

RIGHT CONCENTRATION: focussing on things as they are

Mandala of Chakrasamvara

Mandala of female energy.

19

Mandala of
Guhyasamaja

The King
of Tantra.

20

Mahayana ~ *the medium-level approach*

Mahayana, while not contradicting it, views Hinayana as a selfish approach, limiting our human potential and still containing within itself the seeds of unhappiness. The belief is that you cannot avoid the world as we are all an inseparable part of it. Thus the Mahayana path extends beyond the individual to include the wellbeing of all people through the practice of the Six Perfections Leading to Enlightenment.

The Six Perfections Leading to Enlightenment

Progressing on the path of finding deeper happiness through spiritual method, you realise that you are not independent. Others have a profound impact on the state of your own happiness. While others are miserable around you, you are unlikely to be happy.

As this understanding dawns, you also realise a great deal of gratitude is owed to others for your existence not only during this lifetime but from countless previous lives.

These two realisations drive you to become confident in your own ability to help others. You begin to perfect the practice of generousity, discipline, patience, enthusiasm, concentration and wisdom which produces enlightenment in oneself. This is the true practice of compassion.

Vajrayana ~ the highest-level approach

Vajrayana is based on the Mahayana ideal but goes one step further, recognising that we are not only part of the world but are at one with it. This approach also believes that, in essence, the self is already enlightened because everything good, bad or indifferent in the world does not appear dualistic but is the expression of one's origins of pure mind. Thus one does not wait for enlightenment to occur in the future but through the practice of deity yoga, a process of self-empowerment, one removes self-doubt and arrives at the realisation of enlightenment as being current and immediate in our body, mind and speech.

Duality

In the Tibetan language, duality is literally translated as 'two in one'. Buddhism defines everything within two aspects of reality—ultimate and conventional. Everything that we see and feel is seen as conventionally true and functions accordingly. Yet how we see things is not inherently how they are. This distinction is the nature of duality.

Mahakala. Protector deity of Gyuto Tantric University.
Butter sculpture image created by Thupten Kelsang,
Bonython Hall, University of Adelaide, 1995.

PART 1
Introspection:
the personal journey

Always begin with pure heart
and good motivation.

Happiness is a choice ~
it is your choice.

To seek release from suffering
first know what you want.

𝒴our anger is the basis of your own misery;
it has nothing to do with anyone else.

A good solution is to recognise the problem.

$\mathcal{D}$isappointment is a point on
the path to happiness.

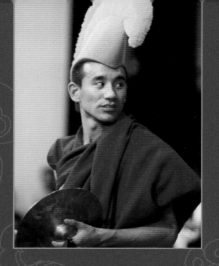

$\mathcal{W}$hen you feel rejected you are a party to a shared understanding ~ don't participate in the projection and you won't feel this way.

$\mathcal{L}$etting go of attachment to pain and hurt creates a path to healing and recovery.

$\mathcal{T}$o see something to forgive is to see blame.

The realisation of nothing to forgive
shows a true recovery from hurt.

$\mathcal{B}$itterness destroys only you,
no-one else.

Peace of mind and happiness
isn't achieved through mindlessness.
Peace of mind, contentment and happiness
arise from the sustained practice of belief
in your own good fortune as a human being,
in maintaining a sense of greater purpose
and in not harming others.

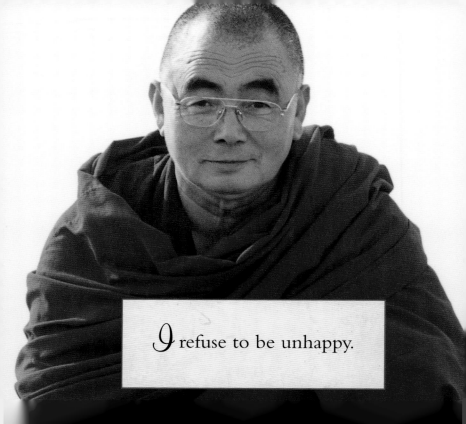

I refuse to be unhappy.

Need rules over doctrine.

Religion is not a degree but
a guide to living our life.
Religion exists to serve us rather
than the other way round.

$\mathcal{Y}$our job is to make yourself happy ~
leave it to others to make you unhappy.

A good start is to assume good.

To be buddhist is to be prepared to accept the consequence of your action.

Only the brave can be non-violent.

$\mathcal{T}$o feel loved is to find spirituality;
to love others is to experience greatness;
to hurt is to prove humanness.

45

Check your motivation all the time.
Good will always prevail, as a muddy stream
will clear, when it comes from a pure source.

46

$\mathcal{I}$mpermanence is hope not annihilation ~ it allows change and possibility.

$\mathcal{A}$ true practitioner of one religion is
a true follower of all religions.

The working of impermanence is
a true display of magic.

PART 2
The practice of
compassion

*G*ood heart and good motivation
keep the mind focussed.

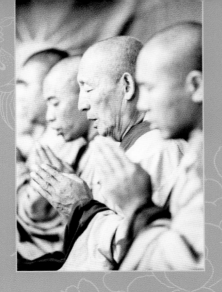

*D*o good because you want to; otherwise
it becomes the practice of resentment.

Right action and right speech
keeps you safe.

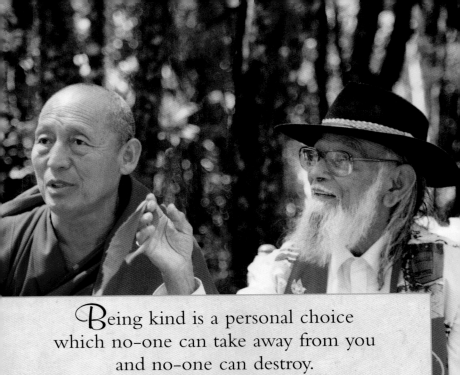

$\mathcal{B}$eing kind is a personal choice
which no-one can take away from you
and no-one can destroy.

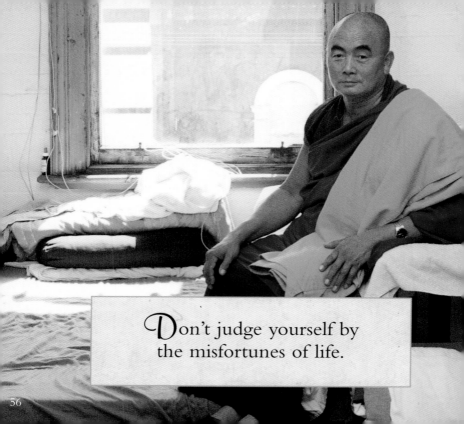

Don't judge yourself by
the misfortunes of life.

Anger is the intent to harm.
There is no such thing as good anger.

To be greedy is to want more
but end up with less.

The biggest contribution to end the world's suffering is to end your own suffering.

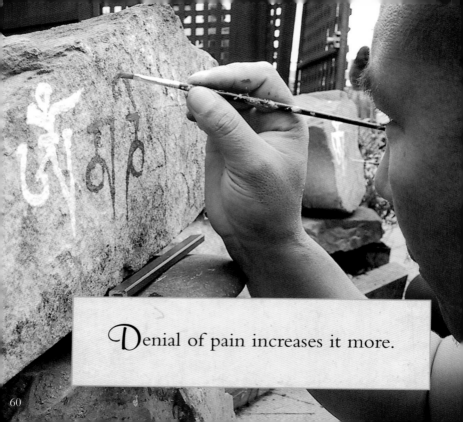

Denial of pain increases it more.

To be bitter is to add weight
to your enemy's arrow.

Good motivation is the best
antidote to disappointment.

When you realise you are not a spectator
on the outside of life, happiness, openness,
and contentment follows.

It is a big heart that feels the suffering of others.

64

To imagine receiving the burdens of others
is not to be overwhelmed but to celebrate
your capacity to care for others.

Charity is in the giving
not in the given.

The limit of compassion is when it destroys your peace of mind.

Ultimate compassion is staying in your own goodness, not cracking under the pressure of provocation or temptation.

The one thing your enemies
can't steal or destroy is your right
to practise compassion.

$\mathcal{T}$he essence of humanity is found in gratitude, grace and confidence.

$\mathcal{W}$hen you are happy you help others more
and stop creating harm and worry for them ~
this is the essence of compassion.

Human affection is the best medicine.

Unconditional love requires
a suspension of judgement.

To believe in universal compassion is to believe in your own humanity.

Compassion builds the confidence to accept
the power of your own self-worth which
is the reflection of enlightenment.

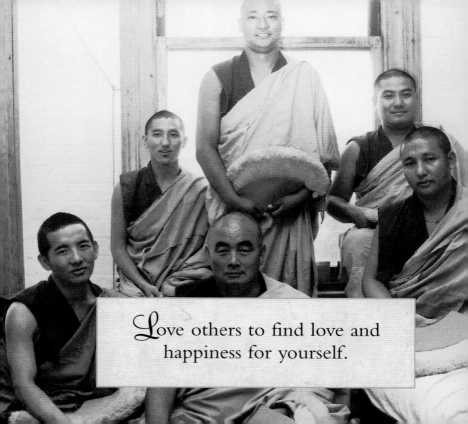

Love others to find love and
happiness for yourself.

Compassion is a can-do attitude.

PART 3

Transformation:
the big picture

It's debatable whether the nature of mind is pure but to believe in it is pure because that belief produces a positive result.

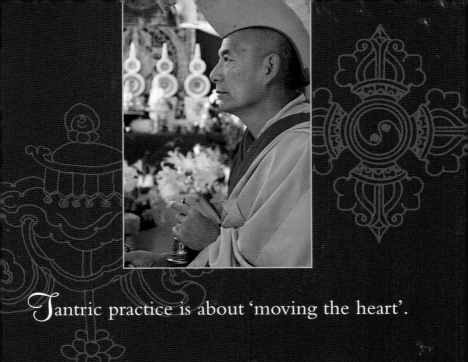

Tantric practice is about 'moving the heart'.

Loss of self-awareness is ego.

The only hiding place for fear is in your own lack of self-esteem.

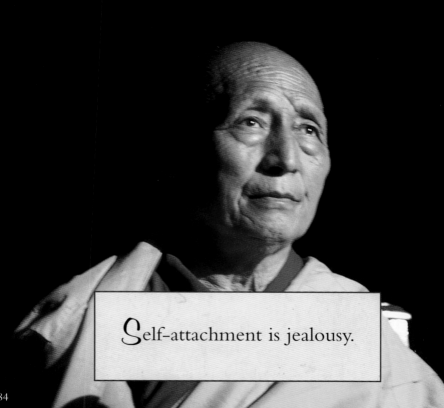

Self-attachment is jealousy.

Self-hatred is the root of suffering.

Healing comes from changing
our perception of suffering.

$\mathcal{I}$t is a greater sacrifice to renounce pain in favour of happiness than to remain in pain.

Self-analysis finds the spiritual destination;
self-embrace makes it home for the
weary mind to rest.

When you know yourself, you are free
for the knower has disappeared.

*L*earned wisdom brings arrogance;
the experience of wisdom brings inner peace.

Spiritual growth only occurs within
the belief of intrinsic goodness.

The Middle Way is not mediocrity or compromise; it is a self-perfected state.

*I*f you see yourself as good
you will see everything as good.

$\mathcal{S}$elf-love is pure love.

Ultimately it is self-doubt that stands between happiness and unhappiness.

95

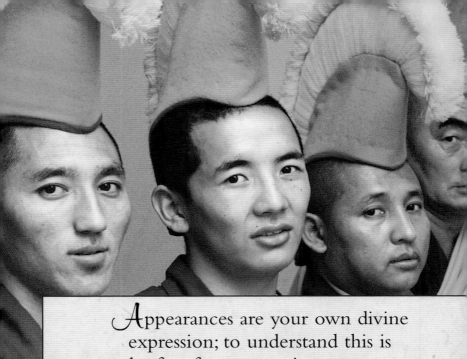

$\mathcal{A}$ppearances are your own divine
expression; to understand this is
to be free from samsaric entrapment.

$\mathcal{E}$nlightenment comes through the balance
of wisdom and compassion, through the
harmony between male and female energies.

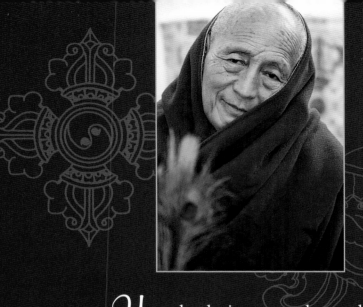

Your body is a sacred mandala.
There is no need to seek external sacred places.

To visualise the mandala is to experience oneself as perfect in a perfect world.

$\mathcal{A}$n end to the spiritual quest is when you realise there is no designated destination.

$\mathcal{A}$ self-respecting person will
never create bad kharma.

𝒴ou are special because
of who you are.

The essence of everthing is emptiness.
Emptiness is pure. You are that purity.

Gyuto Tantric University in Exile in India

The Gyuto Monks live in a remote area of North–East India in the state of Arunachal Pradesh, one of the most inaccessible parts of the country. For some years they have been attempting to relocate the monastery to Dharamsala, home of the Dalai Lama, but scarce resources have delayed significant progress until recently when continuing Australian support for Gyuto Monastery has given the monks the confidence and practical help to forge ahead with building. An exciting stage has now been reached and it is hoped that relocation of the 500 monks to the new premises will begin in 2003. With this move, it will be possible to start addressing health and education needs and to set this very important monastery within the Gelugpa tradition of Tibetan Buddhism on a stable base.

LEFT *Young Refugee Monks of Gyuto outside monastery school.*

RIGHT *Monks entering main 'gompa' or meditation hall, Gyuto Monastery, Arunachal Pradesh.*

ཁྱད་པར་རྒྱུད་སྨད་གྲྭ་ཚང་།

GYUTO TANTRIC UNIVERSITY

LEFT *Learning mandala construction using a mud model prior to progressing to the creation of sand mandalas.*

RIGHT *Chanting meditation inside main 'gompa', Gyuto Monastery, Arunachal Pradesh.*

Support and donations for Gyuto Monastery can be made through Gyuto House Australia or directly to the monastery in India:

Gyuto Tantric
University
Ramoche Temple
PO Sidbhari—176057
Dharamsala
Kangra HP
INDIA

Gyuto House Australia

Gyuto House was established in 1996 following annual visits by the monks to Australia since 1994. Envisaged as a centre without walls, it has fulfilled this vision to the extent that the home base remains an extremely modest property and the monks travel the length and breadth of Australia, responding to invitations to provide cultural programs in a diverse range of settings. Priorities are to cultivate the precious relationship of kindness and compassion being exchanged between the monks and Australians of all ages, beliefs and backgrounds, as well as provide assistance to Gyuto Monastery in India. The warmth and affection, and the generosity of spirit which Gyuto House enjoys from its nation-wide support base, is gratefully acknowledged as an example of community goodness in action.

Gyuto House
Riverside Drive
Second Valley, S.A. 5204
Email gyutoaus@bigpond.com
www.gyuto.va.com.au

New Ramoche at Sidhari near Dharamsala, India—the new Gyuto Tantric University Meditation Hall. The building of monk accommodation will be completed and opened by HH the Dalai Lama in 2003 whereupon the monastic community will relocate from Arunachal Pradesh.

PHOTOGRAPH CREDITS

AUSTRALIAN RECORDINGS BY THE GYUTO MONKS

The Tantric Trilogy: classic harmonic chanting

The Practice of Contentment: a meditation guide

Sounds of Global Harmony: a unique musical collaboration featuring the Gyuto Monks wi Sarah Hopkins on cello, Chris Neville of didgeridoo and Anne Norman on shakuhachi

Om Mani Padre Hum 'The Jewel in the Lotus': a guided meditation for healing the heart.